D1396770

The Well-Traveled Dog

Sandra Gurvis

About the Author

Sandra Gurvis is the author of nine books and hundreds of magazine articles. Her books have been featured in newspapers and on television and radio programs across the country. Sandra has won awards for her writing and is a member of the American Society of Journalists and Authors. She lives in Columbus, Ohio.

T.F.H. Publications, Inc.
One TFH Plaza
Third and Union Avenues
Neptune City, NJ 07753

This book has been published with the intent to provide accurate and authoritative information in regard to the subject matter within. While every precaution has been taken in preparation of this book, the publisher and author assume no responsibility for errors or omissions. Neither is any liability assumed for damages resulting from the use of the information herein.

ISBN 0-7938-3090-7

Printed and bound in the United States of America

Printed and Distributed by T.F.H. Publications, Inc.
Neptune City, NJ

Contents

Introduction

For decades, dogs and cats have been accepted companions in hotels and restaurants abroad, particularly in France where even tourists' canines can gain entrance sans quarantine and many restrictions. Author Peter Mayle even chronicled his overseas adventures with his shaggy canine, Boy, in his bestsellers, *A Year in Provence* and *A Dog's Life*. But until recently in the United States, dogs and their owners were relegated to cheap motels and campgrounds—and even then, they weren't always welcome. Eateries that accommodated Rover were practically nonexistent. Those accompanied by their pets were usually limited to fast-food drive-throughs.

But all of that is changing. According to the American Animal Hospital Association (AAHA), 53 percent of pet owners vacationed or traveled with their animals in 1996. That number shot up to 67 percent in 1998. And by the mid-90's, nearly half of the members of the American Hotel and Motel Association (AHMA) allowed pets, a statistic that seems to be on the rise also, considering the proliferation of lists of "pet friendly" places on web sites and in travel books and magazine articles. The American Automobile Association (AAA) alone has approved more than 10,000 lodgings in the US that welcome canine and other nonhuman companions. Some estimates reach as high as 23,000, including hotels, motels, campgrounds, ranches, and resorts. Perhaps in the not-too-distant future some places will welcome only dogs, provided their owners behave properly.

Nearly half a million dogs and cats fly on major US airlines every year, many in first class or "steerage" with their owners (it beats the cargo hold, where critters may be exposed to extreme temperatures, plane changes where they're handled as baggage, and fluctuations in air pressure). Although the Safe Air Travel for Animals Act, which would have imposed even stricter regulations on air transportation of pets, failed in Congress, recent legislation now requires airlines to make monthly reports on those that are lost, injured, or die. The Animal Welfare Act (AWA) administered by the United States Department of Agriculture–Animal Plant Health Inspection Service (USDA-APHIS) also provides some protection. Airlines that do accept four-legged passengers generally have stringent requirements.

If you must leave your pet at home when traveling, there are numerous options available for care, from first-rate pet sitters to sending your dog on his own holiday.

Thousands of resorts, lodgings, and campgrounds now welcome canine and other nonhuman traveling companions.
Photo courtesy of The Chesterfield Hotel.

This book covers all aspects of the journey—from high fliers to the back roads, luxury resorts and "ruffing" it in the campgrounds, and all points in between. Quality options are even available for those who prefer to leave their critters behind or send them on their own holiday. Along with suggestions and basic rules, accessories that make the trip easier are also included.

"Seven out of ten Americans think of their pets as children," stated Marty Becker, co-author of *Chicken Soup for the Dog Lover's Soul* in a recent issue of *National Geographic Traveler*. So it's no wonder that more and more destinations are making room for Rover.

Road Trips with Your Dog

Canines generally love to travel and accompany their owners on trips more than any other animal. And they're usually the most adaptable of our four-legged companions; even felines often become bent out of shape with any change in environment. Like humans, dogs relish new scenery and car rides, particularly if they're sitting next to their favorite person or family in the world.

Should You Take Your Dog?

Before making that first reservation, consider whether Rover is up to the trip. Is he very young (8 weeks to 4 months) or old (over 10 years), pregnant, sick, or given to biting or barking? Does he have difficulty with obedience? If the answer is yes to any of these questions, then you might want to reconsider. Not only should Rover be able to respond to such voice commands as "Sit," "Stay," and "Down," but he must be socialized and relaxed enough to react positively to unfamiliar people and situations, including other dogs and possibly even cats.

Other factors should be considered as well. If the dog is prone to motion sickness, make sure you have proper medication in the right dosage on hand at all times. A 35-pound black Labrador Retriever, for instance, is going to need a stronger prescription than a toy Poodle. Consult your veterinarian about various options. Some doctors may even recommend a mild tranquilizer so Rover doesn't become overstimulated and pee on the antique chair in the lobby while you're checking in.

Additionally, the dog should be crate trained. Generally, this begins in puppyhood, so he is familiar and content inside an enclosed space and knows that's where he's to be quiet, sleep, and, in general, behave. It's also a sort of home away from home, and if lodgings know that you're bringing along a crate or carrier, they'll be more likely to accept your pooch. Some hotels may even allow

Photo courtesy of Rovin' with Rover.

Before deciding to take your dog on a trip, make sure he is up to it. He should be able to respond to basic commands and socialized and relaxed enough to react positively in unfamiliar situations.

you to leave the dog alone in a crate for short periods of time; check with the management before doing so, however. The carrier also eliminates the potentially dangerous distraction of having the dog running free in the car. You may want to invest in a doggie seatbelt harness; some cars actually come equipped with them, or they can be purchased independently.

The vacation will be a bummer if there's no place for Rover to come along. Some places such as Hilton Head and Myrtle Beach have multitudinous restrictions against pets, while others like Key West and Carmel-by-the-Sea in California are considered top destinations by canine cognoscenti. Recreation areas in Georgia, ski resorts in Colorado and Stowe, Vermont (keep Rover on closed lifts only), and even big cities like San Francisco and New Orleans welcome the scratch-and-sniff set. Many dog-friendly hotels are located within walking distance of outdoor attractions, and sometimes even museums and art galleries allow well-behaved pets. Overseas travel can be fraught with complications, although trips to Canada and Mexico are doable, as long as you are aware of and follow each country's regulations.

Information on Traveling with Your Dog

Many of these web sites provide up-to-date information on pet-friendly lodgings (by state), places to go, and things to do with your dog, as well as suggestions for restaurants and other geographical areas that are particularly amenable to canines. You might want to visit more than one; for instance, healthypet.com is the official site for the American Animal Hospital Association (AAHA) and offers medical information, while petplanet.com covers all aspects of ownership for a variety of critters. Sites particular to dogs include dogfriendly.com and travel-dog.com. And although it's not on the web, the American Automobile Association (AAA) publishes a detailed guide, *Traveling With Your Pet: The AAA Petbook*, available to members at most local offices. 888/Inn-Seek (888/466-7335, www.inseek.com) has a toll-free listing of pet-friendly lodgings.

TRAVEL:

companimalz.com
dogfriendly.com
doggonefun.com
interpetexplorer.com
petlifeweb.com
petplanet.com
petsonthego.com
petswelcome.com
petvacations.com
takeyourpet.com
thedogpark.com
traveldog.com
travellingpet.com
travelpets.com

MEDICAL:

avma.org (American Veterinary Animal Association)
healthypet.com (American Animal Hospital Association)

(All sites prefaced by "http://www."unless otherwise noted.)

Preparing for the Trip

A journey of just a few miles begins with a single paw print, and planning ahead is essential for a successful canine-companion vacation. You can make the task easier by always mentioning that you'll have one or more dogs with you when making reservations. Even the most pet-friendly hotels can change management and no longer allow four-legged companions. Also, find out what other places at your destination welcome dogs and if there are any nearby parks and beaches that you both can visit.

Always ask about the lodging's policy regarding pets, if a deposit is required, and if there's a place for exercise. It might also be wise to request a room at the end of the hall and away from heavy traffic areas, such as near the lobby, ice machine, elevators, or pool. (Some establishments even have special rooms designated for dogs and their owners.) Should Rover begin to yap, there will be fewer complaints. If your dog does bark a lot, you'll need to figure out a way to keep it to a low roar, either by keeping him with you at a111l times or giving him a mild tranquilizer (with your vet's approval, of course) for the hour or two that you might need to leave him alone. The first floor is also good when the urge for an outside purge becomes immediate.

Make sure that your dog is in top health, that he's clean and flea-free, and that his vaccinations are up to date. This might also include a shot against bordetella (kennel cough) and preventative medication for heartworm. If applicable, take plenty of his required medication. Like other doctors, veterinarians must see the animal first before writing any prescription; this simple precaution saves inconvenience, trouble, and money at your destination. If your dog had a past history of sickness, have your home vet check him out beforehand, even if he's currently feeling fine. Bring along a copy of his medical records just in case.

Investigate the potential hazards of where you're going, as well. For instance, there may be quarantines outside the US, and certain parts of the country, such as Florida, have alligators that may like to snack on Rover or heartworm-carrying mosquitoes. Mountainous and wooded areas may be infested with ticks that transmit Lyme disease. The latter vary from year to year, so check with AAA or a travel agent.

Planning ahead is essential for a successful canine-companion vacation. When making arrangements, confirm that your hotel and places at your destination, like nearby parks and beaches, welcome dogs.

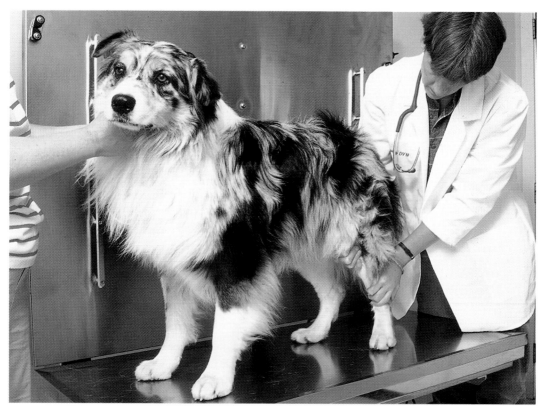

In preparation for a trip, your dog should be in top health, he should be clean and flea-free, and his vaccinations should be up to date.

If Rover's not used to traveling in a car, make a few short trial runs to see how he adapts to the experience. Many dogs associate car rides with trips to the vet and might initially freak out. It might also be wise to expose your dog to brief doses of crowds, noise, elevators, and stairs.

On the day of departure, wait at least four hours after the last feeding/watering before leaving. You might want to keep towels and moisture wipes on hand in case of motion sickness. And just before you put the key in the ignition, give him a long walk so he can relieve himself and be accident-free and refreshed for the journey ahead.

What to Take

❖ Food. "Pack just enough to get to your destination, then purchase more once you've arrived," advises Wendy Ballard, publisher of *DogGone Newsletter*, a bimonthly publication that focuses on canine travel. Don't forget a can opener and a spoon; otherwise, you may have a hungry pup and no way to get to his meal.

❖ Water. "Bring some from home to ease your pet's transitions to 'vacation water,'" she continues. "The last thing you want is a dog with an upset tummy." Gradually introduce the new water source. Bottled water is also generally a safe bet, and a spray bottle or "zipper"-type plastic bags filled with water are convenient founts when you're on the road.

❖ Plastic (or otherwise unbreakable) dishes for the above.

❖ Leash. Most places have leash laws, and constant and consistent use prevents the night-marish dilemma of having the dog bolt away from you in a strange place.

❖ Identification tags. Worn at all times, these may include a license plate and ID tag listing your dog's name and yours. You can also have the animal tattooed with an ID number (usually a Social Security number), or have a microchip implanted. If the dog requires special medication/treatment, that info should be on the collar as well.

❖ An extra flea/tick collar.

❖ Crate. This is essential for any type of travel, be it on the ground or in the air.

❖ Scooping materials and plastic bags for waste. Your pooch is an ambassador of sorts and you only want him spreading good will.

❖ Grooming aids. Regular brushing will "keep shedding to a minimum," says Ballard. "Hotel maids will appreciate it."

❖ Carpet deodorizer and cleaner (in case accidents do occur).

❖ Dog towel or blanket. This will prove useful in keeping hair off both the car and the bed-spread. It also doubles as a wipe for Rover and his feet after the "dewy morning walk or dip in the lake," adds Ballard.

❖ Medication—enough for the trip—and a first aid kit. The latter is particularly helpful in removing ticks. Ticks are often found in heavily wooded areas and can be picked up during hikes, so carefully inspect your dog afterward.

❖ Toys and treats. "You pet's favorite chewie or stuffed animal helps make him feel at home no matter where he is," says Ballard.

❖ Proof of vaccination. Some states require documentation on current rabies shots before the dog can enter their borders. If you're traveling to Canada or Mexico, he will need a health certificate.

Rules of the Car

We've all seen the pooch with his head out the car window, sitting unencumbered in the front seat with a big grin on his face. Some dogs even roam free in the bed of a truck and look like they're having a terrific time. What a carefree way to start your vacation!

But would you permit your children to engage in these activities or partake in them yourself? Like people, dogs are susceptible to flying debris from the road and other vehicles, as well as being thrown through the windshield during sudden stops. That is why experts such as the American Animal Hospital Association (AAHA) and the American Society for the Prevention of Cruelty to Animals (ASPCA) recommend some form of restraint, be it a specially designed seatbelt harness or a car seat for smaller pets. Windows should be kept closed enough so that the dog keeps his snout in the car; running the air conditioner/heater might be the best solution.

Adjustable leashes that can be attached to truck beds are also available; however, riding in the bed of a pickup is illegal in some states. Even tethered dogs can be dragged along the road in the event that they try to jump out; the pooch could become entangled in the straps and accidentally strangle him-self. You might not realize you've seriously injured or even lost your best friend until you reach your destination. A dog should also not be allowed to roam in campers or recreational vehicles unless they're parked and set up for the night.

The most common and flexible option is a crate or carrier. Not only does it permit portability—it goes wherever you do—but it prevents Rover from chewing on your leather interior or attempting to make a dash for freedom when you open the door. Crates should allow for ventilation and plenty of extra space, so that Rover can sit, stand, turn around and lie down. The crate should also be lined with blankets or towels for comfort and to absorb accidents. Make sure you have plenty of extra towels on hand; also include toys to keep your dog entertained.

It may be cute to see two doggies sitting in the front seat of an empty car, looking as if they're about to drive off, but even one dog left alone can be an invitation to disaster. Not only might Rover accidentally put

A crate is essential for any type of travel. Also, if lodgings know you are bringing along a crate or carrier, they will be more likely to accept your pooch.

the vehicle in gear, but a rolled-down window opens up the possibility for theft. Perhaps more importantly, leaving your dog alone for even a short time can result in hypothermia from the cold or heatstroke. Cranking down the windows and popping up the sunroof do little to reduce the temperature on a warm day and provide a possible avenue of escape.

Other common-sense principles apply. Take exercise breaks every two or so hours so both you and your charge remain fresh and alert. Rest stops are great places for a drink of cool water, a short walk, and chance for everyone to use the facilities. And before exiting the car, make sure "Houdini's" leash is firmly attached to his collar to prevent him from escaping. When arriving at your destination, find a peaceful spot so the "great one" can become accustomed to his new environment, even if it's only for a few minutes.

When Out and About

The leash rule applies everywhere you go, unless you're in the hotel room or inside a private residence where you and your four-legged companion are staying. Otherwise, you risk having your pet lost, hurt, or killed. Not everyone has the same affection for canines, especially large, imposing ones.

The leash rule applies everywhere you go with your dog, unless you're in a hotel room or inside a private residence. Otherwise, you risk having your pet lost or hurt.

The approach of a strange unleashed dog can be a recipe for disaster, particularly if smaller critters or kids are involved. Children often feel no compunction about accosting unfamiliar animals; so always be on the lookout, even when Rover's on a tether. A shorter leash allows for more control as well

Restaurants

Eating out with Rover might be easier than you think. "First, ask your pet-loving friends and family for recommendations," writes Heather Walters, author of *Take Your Pet Along* and *Take Your Pet, Too,* guidebooks on PetPlanet.com. "Then look for restaurants with outdoor seating." That way, he will be less likely to bother other patrons. "If the... owner or manager says 'No' just thank [him] and move on. It does you and your pet no good if you become belligerent." Those with more than two dogs might have a more difficult time finding places to eat, however. Drive-through establishments are another alternative.

Stores

Before entering the emporium, make sure that Rover has relieved himself. You don't want any unplanned purchases for something he might ruin. A visit to a pet store before going on the trip is a good idea. Such places are usually forgiving should an accident occur (always offer to clean up the mess, no matter where you are). If he behaves himself there, he'll likely be fine elsewhere.

Walters recommends that you check out what's inside the store to determine whether it's dog-appropriate. If food is being sold or served, Board of Health rules generally prohibit animals from entering. Other no-nos include shops that peddle little or breakable items or if the establishment is small, crowded, or otherwise cramped. "Big stores have more room for your pooch on a leash," she continues, while less traffic-intensive enterprises might welcome "a potential buyer with a best friend on his/her arm."

Parks, Beaches, and Other Public Places

Many festivals and outdoor areas prohibit dogs because they "do their business" where someone might sit or walk. So if you're admitted, make sure your pooch is a shining example of self-control. According to Walters, most beaches have the US Army "Don't ask, don't tell" rule when it comes to Rover, so "if you sneak [in] your dog...after hours or before the sun bathers arrive, nobody's the wiser." (Again, always scoop so as not to ruin this unspoken conspiracy.) Before entering the beach,

Rover Escapes! What To Do?

The following suggestions have been adapted from *The AAA Petbook:*

- ❖ Make sure the dog always wears a sturdy collar with rabies tags and ID, including your home address and phone number.

- ❖ Take along a recent picture and detailed description; this will be helpful in identifying your pet.

- ❖ Immediately contact local police, animal control, and other shelters and veterinary clinics in the area. Provide copies of the above-mentioned photo/description. Stay in constant touch with them and give a number where you can be reached at all times.

- ❖ Post signs around the area and ads in local newspapers, including your phone number, the dog's identifying features, and a picture whenever feasible.

- ❖ Most pets are found within a week, although it can take longer, even several months. And there are those extraordinary (but true) tales of animals who somehow find their way home. The important thing is to keep trying!

however, look for the posted regulations to ensure you're not violating any local laws. Also, many locations have what's known as dog beaches or dog parks where canines can romp freely. All it takes is a little research before you leave to sniff these out.

When out and about, your dog should always wear a sturdy collar with rabies tags and an ID that shows your home address, phone number, and the dog's name—especially when you are far from home.

Even a slight change in diet and water can cause your dog's stomach to become upset, so always bring pet food from home when you travel.

Attractions

The same rules of etiquette apply to attractions, including museums and cultural events. Always call ahead and ask permission. Comments Walters, "You could be pleasantly surprised," especially if they are held outdoors. And if even they don't admit dogs, bigger places like Disney World and Epcot Center have kennels so your pet is cared for in a safe environment.

Keeping Your Dog Healthy During the Trip

Even a slight change in food and water can set off a bout of diarrhea or other stomach upset. So although you've brought enough provisions for the vacation, experimenting with the area's cuisine—which may contain spices, oils, sugars, vegetables, and even liquids unfamiliar to your dog's system—can result in disastrous consequences. Think twice even before giving him a taste; and it goes without saying that dogs should never have chocolate, which can be fatal. Should Rover be feeling deprived, have plenty of her special doggie treats from home at the ready so he can partake safely.

Avoid hypothermia and heatstroke. Strenuous exercise outside during the sunniest hours (10 am–2 pm) can result in the latter, while even walking on a hot beach can blister paws. Signs of heatstroke include rapid, shallow breathing, excessive salivation and panting, high body temperature (hot to the touch), glazed eyes, unsteadiness, deep red or purple tongue or gums, and vomiting. Making sure the dog has plenty of cool, fresh (not salt) water.

Keeping your dog in the shade can help prevent heatstroke, while hypothermia can be circumvented by limiting excursions in colder weather or water. Symptoms include shivering, weakness, lethargy, and being chilly to the touch. After wrapping him in a towel or blanket, place your dog in a warm area, gently messaging his head, chest, and extremities.

According to the American Veterinary Medical Association (AVMA), a doctor should be consulted if your pet shows any of the following signs:

- ❖ Abnormal discharges from the nose, eyes, or other body openings.
- ❖ Lumps, limping, or difficulty getting up or lying down.
- ❖ Loss of appetite, marked weight losses or gains, or excessive water consumption.
- ❖ Difficult, irregular, or uncontrolled waste elimination.
- ❖ Excessive head shaking, scratching, and licking or biting any part of the body.
- ❖ Dandruff, loss of hair, open sores, and a ragged or dull coat.
- ❖ Foul breath or excessive tartar deposits on teeth.

First Aid for Dogs

A first-aid kit is essential, particularly if you're in a remote area where you may not be able to quickly get to a veterinarian. You also need to know how to use it. Guides such as *Pet First Aid: Cats & Dogs* published by the Humane Society of the US (HSUS) and the American Red Cross and *Dog First Aid* by Randy Acker, D.V. M. can assist with short-term care. Nothing is as effective, however, as professional medical attention, particularly if the condition persists. You can assemble your own kit with the following items:

- ❖ gauze
- ❖ bandages and adhesive tape
- ❖ towels
- ❖ hydrogen peroxide
- ❖ rubbing alcohol
- ❖ ointment
- ❖ muzzle
- ❖ scissors
- ❖ tweezers (for removing ticks, burrs, splinters, etc.).

What to Do If Your Dog Becomes Ill

- ❖ Contact the American Animal Hospital Association (AAHA, 800/252-2242, www.healthypet.com). Open from 9 am to 5 pm mountain time, they'll provide you with the location and phone of the nearest affiliated clinic.
- ❖ Should your pet become sick at odd hours, check with the hotel or the Yellow Pages for the closet emergency veterinary hospital. Most cities have at least one facility that offers 24-hour help, although you may have to pay twice the normal rate.
- ❖ Whichever place you choose, make sure it meets your standards in terms of cleanliness and professionalism. Inquire about fees before committing to a course of treatment.
- ❖ Have your current veterinarian's phone number handy so the clinic can call and get medical records, if necessary.

Hotels and Special Getaways

Staying in a hotel can be fun for everyone, as long as your best friend is welcome, too. Web sites provide state-by-state listings of hotels that accept dogs. Publications such as the *DogGone Newsletter* (561/569-8434) and *AAA Petbook,* as well as guidebooks like *The Dog Lovers Companion Series* (800/364-4676) and *On the Road Again With Man's Best Friend* (available from bookstores) will help you dig for the best places. Certain chain hotels may also accommodate Rover as well, although, as discussed earlier, it's always best to get in touch with each lodging regarding specific policies. Along with having strict requirements as to size and number of dogs, some may require a pet deposit, part of which may be nonrefundable.

Hotel Petiquette

When staying away from home, dogs need to be on their best behavior. The following are some common-sense tips that will make your hotel visit easier and pave the way for other four-legged guests, as well as inviting a return performance.

❖ Before bringing Rover into the lobby, ask the clerks if he is allowed there, otherwise things might get off to an awkward start.

❖ Dog-proof the room. Check for such hazards as chemically-treated toilet water, electrical cords, hiding spaces, and items the little devil might chew on or otherwise damage. Put anything dangerous out of his reach, along with spreading a blanket over the bedspread to avoid the "cashmere effect." Bring favorite toys from home so he can remain occupied.

❖ If accidents do occur, mop them up using your own sanitizing solution and paper towels, not the hotel's.

Dogs need to be on their best behavior when staying away from home. Always dog-proof the hotel room as best you can and bring some of your pooch's favorite toys so he can remain occupied while you're out.

- ❖ If you groom or bathe the dog in the room, clean up the mess, including all excess hair in the bathroom.

- ❖ Some experts recommend never leaving your pooch alone in a hotel room, that it may, in some instances, invite dognapping. To help keep your dog quiet and well-behaved, however, you might be able to crate him for short periods. This way, "your pet won't scare, harass or—worse—bite the maids," says Wendy Ballard of the *DogGone Newsletter*. "This also decreases the chance that Sneaky Pete will slip out the door."

- ❖ When you do leave the dog alone, always crate him. Let the management know, and provide a phone number where you can be reached if there's an incident or barking.

- ❖ When in the room with the dog, always place a "do not disturb" sign on the door and keep the deadbolt locked so as not to startle the housekeepers.

- ❖ On the other hand, arrange for housekeeping when both you and your dog are out of the room. The first night, leave a nice tip and note thanking the cleaner. A little extra cash for each day's stay goes a long way toward engendering goodwill.

- ❖ Make sure the dog relieves himself away from the shrubs near the rooms, where other patrons might step (owners

Pet-Friendly Chain Hotels

Comfort Inns—800-221-2222
Days Inn—800-329-746
Howard Johnson—800-446-4656
La Quinta Inns—800-531-5900
Red Roof Inns—800-843-7663
Residence Inn—800-331-3131
Super 8 Motels—800-800-8000
Westin Hotels—800-228-3000

can only pooper scoop so much). Bushes in the parking lot might be the best places for a quick pee.

❖ Allow your pet only in designated exercise or animal-approved areas; other public places like the lobby, pool, restaurant, and patio may be off-limits.

❖ Before checking out, make sure there's no evidence that Rover has been there. Carefully inspect the room for damage. If there is destruction, honesty is the best policy. It beats getting an unpleasant surprise on your credit card bill a few weeks later that might include not only the pet deposit fee but charges for additional repairs as well.

City Dog: Jumping Into the Lap of Luxury

Certain hotels are famous for their hospitality toward canines. Although they may take a bite out of the budget, the old Mark Twain axiom applies: You get what you pay for. The following is a partial list of some well-known establishments that welcome Rover with open arms—and lots more. Many are located close to downtown and attractions, so you and your pet can visit various sites on foot.

The Alexis Hotel, Seattle, WA, 800/426-7033. For a small fee per stay, Rover gets a "deluxe doggie upgrade." This includes a keepsake water bowl with distilled water, complimentary pet treats, and perhaps the most valuable of all, a copy of *Seattle Dog-Lovers Companion* to assist you both in your travels. Your dog also has his very own designer bed, in addition to a morning and afternoon walk by an Alexis bellman. Along with a "doggie room service menu," His Dogginess can be treated to a rubdown from a masseuse specializing in pets, as well as sessions with an animal psychologist (to overcome the trauma of the trip, perhaps?). Goodies for owners include turndown service with chocolates, terrycloth bathrobe during the stay, private steam and fitness facilities, along with a variety of room styles, including fireplace, spa, and executive suites.

The Chesterfield, Palm Beach, CA, 800/243-7871. Considering that nearby Worth Avenue has a special "dog bar," a tiled trough with a silver spigot for Rover to quench his thirst; that local stores sell Chanel dog collars and Gucci pooch beds; and that this hotel hosts a Pet

Upon arrival, inform yourself of the lodging's requirements regarding pets. Allow your dog only in designated animal-approved areas; some public places like the lobby, restaurant, and patio may be off-limits.

Fashion Show replete with the latest designs, you might get reverse sticker shock when you learn that rooms are affordable and that your dog can stay free at this small but elegantly refurbished rococo jewel. This may have something to do with the fact that Lucy, a Chinese Shar-Pei, manages the front desk under the aegis of being the GM's pet. The lucky dog (or two, if you stay in a suite) gets his own bed, toys and treats upon arrival, food and water dishes, a pet room service menu, and access (with owner) to pool-side or courtyard dining. This British-owned hotel—which also hosts two-legged celebrities—also boasts the historic Leopard Lounge and Supper Club, a draw for the local moneyed set (what other kind is there around these parts?) and a gen-u-ine afternoon English Tea.

The Colonnade Hotel, Boston, MA, 800/962-3030. Located in Back Bay area near downtown Boston, or "The Hub" (as in of the universe) as the natives like to refer to it, this posh lodging has 285 guest rooms in a variety of styles and amenities. What makes it particularly appealing to pet owners is the friendly staff and the fact that special "Cause for Paws Weekend Packages" welcome animal owners and contribute a percentage of the proceeds to the Massachusetts Society for the Prevention of Cruelty to Animals (MSPCA). You and your canine can enjoy specially designed rooms and treats, including breakfast for two at the hotel's Brasserie Jo. You might want to share the complimentary bottle of champagne with a human companion, however.

Loews Hotels: L'Enfant Plaza, Washington, DC, 202/484-1000; Coronado Bay Resort, Coronado, CA 619/424-4000. An active participant in the "Loews Loves Pets" program, the L'Enfant Plaza, located in the business and historic district of DC, hosts a VIP (Very Important Pet) program that includes a passport stamped with a paw print for each stay. Accumulate five of these and get a free weekend night. Your pampered canine receives dog bones and a special water bowl on a silver tray, while 5 percent of the room rate goes to less fortunate creatures at the Second Chance Wildlife Center. The Loews Coronado Bay Resort donates even more—10 percent of the cost of the lodging—to the Helen Woodward Animal Shelter. They also provide plenty of suggestions as to "pet-friendly" activities and beaches in the San Diego area. Pets are always welcome at Loews properties, including the House of Blues Hotel in Chicago, the Regency Hotel in New York, and the Loews Giorgio Hotel in Denver. Many host fund-raising events for four-legged causes and other special activities.

The Regal Maxwell House Hotel, Nashville, TN, 800/457-4460. This hotel even has its own Very Important Pet (VIP) Web page (www.maxwellhousehotel.com), which features the latest, er, poop on guest and "employee" dogs and cats. With a spectacular view of the skyline, the entire third floor is reserved for pets and there's a dedicated area for dog walking. The staff even cleans up the mess! Along with the human luxuries of lighted tennis courts, swimming pools, indoor exercise rooms, whirlpool, and—a real bonus for anyone who's ever stayed downtown—free parking, the hotel offers a pet amenity menu through room service. Also, be prepared to encounter the hotel's other four-legged workers: Rusty, the Sheltie "bellman;" Starbuck, the Chief of Security who also happens to be a Weimaraner; and the feline Spuds, a sort of lifeguard in that she lounges frequently by the pool. While in the exercise room, you might also see the canine Rambo, enjoying the treadmill, "but not if it goes too fast."

The Ritz-Carlton, Chicago, IL, 800/621-6906. They don't say it "putting on the Ritz" for nothing. Guest doggies get a welcome gift of fancy food and biscuits; along with a "gour-r-met room service

Before checking out, make sure there's no evidence that your dog has been there. Clean up any doggie messes and carefully inspect the room for damage; this paves the way for future canine guests. Photo courtesy of Alexis Hotel.

menu" featuring items from (egad!) Beluga Caviar with or without garnish to more wallet-friendly "Canine Classics" chopped filet mignon and grilled breast of chicken. The good news is that the caviar is offered to cats, so Rover probably won't be interested. The concierge provides dog walking, and a "pet corner" in the hotel shop peddles leashes, treats, and designer duds. The in-house kennel offers a full range of grooming services—shampoo, haircut, nail clipping, ear cleaning, etc.—by appointment only, of course. And if your dog is celebrating a special occasion, let the staff know so they can prepare a surprise (yours might be on the bill).

The SoHo Grand Hotel, New York, NY, 800/965-3000; TriBeCa Grand Hotel, New York, NY, 877/519-6600. Now visitors to the Big Apple have two pet-friendly hotels to choose from, both owned by Hartz Mountain Industries. The vast range of a la carte offerings consist of in-room dining, assorted toys, full body pillow, vitamins, even toothbrush and toothpaste for that important meeting with the puppy next door. Options abound for grooming and care, including in-room vet calls, walking, pet sitting, or even overnight boarding. Discriminating pooches can choose between a complete makeover at "Doggie-Do and Pussycats, Too!" or a "master" (i.e., do-it-yourself) clean at the Beverly Hills Laundermutt. Pet taxi, chauffeur, and limo service are also available. Oh, and if you can't take your four-legged companion along on vacation, the hotel will provide a goldfish to keep you company (those who get attached can bring home the fish with an instructional brochure). Over 25 percent of the Grand Hotel's 369 rooms are available to critters and receive specialized cleaning. The brand-new TriBeCa offers the same pet amenities, but is slightly more expensive.

Country Dog: The Paws that Refresh

Not just big cities roll out the "welcome mutt." Smaller resorts, hotels, and bed and breakfasts offer specialized services and can be (but aren't always) less expensive, providing an array of activities for both of you. Many areas are peppered with these out-of-the-way places known mostly to locals and dog aficionados. So take a lesson from your best friend and keep your ears perked up for recommendations, including the following:

Gray Eagle Lodge, Graeagle, CA, 800/635-8778. DogFriendly.com's "Pick of the Month," this isolated establishment offers TV and phone-free cabins in the beautiful Sierra Mountains. You and Rover can hike on well-marked trails or relax by one of 40 alpine lakes and fish. Not only will the kitchen pack you a picnic lunch, but they'll clean and cook your catch. However, "keep in mind Chef's largest frying pan is only 24 inches wide!" states the Web site. Evenings can be spent playing fetch or, if your dog allows it, cards and ping-pong (as long as he can chase the balls). There is a two-pet limit per cabin and you must sign a pet policy form upon arrival.

Inn by the Sea, Cape Elizabeth, ME, 800/888-4287. Studded with the AAA's Four Diamond and the Mobile Four Star designations, this gracious sprawl provides four-legged guests with a tag bearing the hotel's name and phone number. Brandy also receives a welcome snack and evening turndown treats. Other bounties include complimentary bones, dog dishes, and pooper-scoopers (with the management's strong encouragement to use them). After an afternoon romp in the ocean, he can dry off in the hotel's soft, fluffy towels or play in the property's fenced-in area, although he must be leashed at all other times. Along with Thanksgiving, Christmas, and even Fourth of July offerings, the gourmet menu has everything from hamburgers to chicken to hot dogs, although you might not want to call it that in front of your canine. Top it off with ice cream and a gourmet doggie bon bon. Pet sitting and walking are available so you can enjoy golfing, scuba diving, kayaking, and sunset cruises.

Katherine's House Bed and Breakfast, Mammoth Lakes, CA, 760/934-2991. Those looking to get away from it all will find that the proprietor, Katherine Carter and her mixed-breed, Cleo, are eager to host you and your canine. "We will pamper your best friends while you are out pampering yourself," she states. This vintage chalet-style B&B in a quiet, pine-laden residential neighborhood offers a selection of rooms, suites, and cabins and lots of personalized attention, including coffee or tea service brought to you each morning, full breakfast "when you are ready," plus evening wine and gourmet hors d'oeuvres, along with use of the kitchen. Primo skiing at the Sherwin Mountain Range is a five-minute drive. And not to worry about your companion while you're away: "We love other dogs and will be glad to give them the best of care, including bones, walks and love." Cleo even willingly shares her toys.

The Lorelei Resort, Treasure Island, FL, 800/354-6364. "Pets Stay Free!" declares the sign outside this establishment. That means in-room pet sitting, too. Some out-of-town services are available and with St. Petersburg and Tampa a short ride away—and Disney about a 90-minute drive—this saves money so you can spend more on shopping, touring, and treats for your canine buddy. Also, be aware that most local beaches do not allow pets, so you'll have to leave Rover at the hotel. Nevertheless, with painted-on paw prints at the entrance gate and a fake fire hydrant, these rooms and apartments have really "gone to the dogs." Along with ceramic tile floors (the better to clean up accidents) and kitchens and/or kitchenettes, the Lorelei has a fenced-in patio, a dogs-only swim platform, and easy access to a bay on the property for that early morning dip with your best friend. Leash rules are relaxed as long as the four-legged guests behave; rags, bags, and pooper scoops are also readily available. And in addition to lots of suggestions as to nearby pet-friendly restaurants and parks, there's a groom mobile and pet photographer available. They also have a 24-hour on-call vet. Such a deal!

San Ysidro Ranch, Montecito, CA, 800/368-6788. Talk about a dog's life. This exclusive resort's "Privileged Pet" program starts with a personalized nameplate (his and yours) on your cottage and proceeds to a steak-shaped bed loaded with cookies, toys, and "Pawier" water. You can enjoy a massage alongside your dog, although you might want to choose between the relaxing "slow and gentle," said to increase circulation, or the more rigorous "authentic Reiki," purported to align Zeus's energies by zeroing in on twelve body points. Your dog can then choose from chopped beef with a rawhide shoe or real meat raviolis, along with other items on his special menu. Oh, and there's stuff for you too: walks in the flower gardens and citrus groves on 500 beautifully wooded acres, an ocean view pool, tennis courts, and more. Although dogs are only

Along with providing pet-friendly accommodations, some resorts offer plenty for your dog to explore, like hiking trails along the beach or through wooded parks, personalized exercise and grooming sessions, and fenced-in patios with dogs-only swim areas. Photo courtesy of DogGone Newsletter.

allowed in the free-standing cottages (out of respect for the privacy of other paying guests), grooming and day care are available, along with the services of a local veterinarian.

Stanford Inn by the Sea, Mendocino, CA, 800/331-8884. Long-time innkeepers Joan and Jeff Stanford have always welcomed pets, often finding them better behaved than children. Consisting also of a working organic garden and farm, this wholesome site offers a green-house-enclosed pool, sauna, and spa; a well-equipped fitness center; and panoramic views of pastures, the ocean, and nearby Mendocino. So it should come as no surprise that the Ravens restaurant is vegetarian and smoking is forbidden. Upon being greeted with a biscuit, Rover is provided with dishes for water and food, while owners are given special bags for cleaning up and pet sheets for covering furniture. There's also plenty for your dog to explore: trails along the bay area, as well as parts of nearby Headlands State Park and Big River Beach. The inn offers specially outfitted canoes, with wide beams and carpeting that make it safe and easy for your dog to move around while floating along the Big River Estuary. You get to come along, too.

The Ultimate Getaway: Las Ventanas Resort, Los Cabos, Mexico

Described by the *DogGone Newsletter* as the "quintessential luxury vacation [for] lap-sized Lhasas to Labradors," according to editor Wendy Ballard, Las Ventanas al Paraiso at the tip of Mexico's Baja peninsula lives up to its translation of "windows on paradise." Furnished in Mediterranian-Mexican style architecture, suites have splash-pools and jacuzzis, telescopes for romantic nighttime viewing, terra cota fireplaces, and some rooftop patios. Sea, mountains, and desert serve as a counterpoint for the area's natural beauty.

Some hotels are famous for their hospitality toward canine guests. Your dog could have his very own designer bed, an afternoon and evening walk with a bellman, and pet room service. Photo courtesy of DogGone Newsletter.

"The pampering started with airport pickup," she recalls. "Not only did the driver bring iced towels and bottled water for us humans, he poured Evian into bone shaped dishes" for her two pooches, Sparky and Iggy. Other four-legged delights included "care packages" filled with treats and rawhide chews, a personalized "paw print" welcome note from the manager, and free run of the property (leashed, of course).

"The poolside staff was very accommodating, breaking out the...bowls for bottled water and providing a pet cabana for shade," continues Ballard. Although she advises against doggy dips in the public area, some suites have a private pool, ideal for canines that enjoy a swim. Dogs are permitted to be walked in the desert countryside and on fine-sand beaches by either resort personnel or owners, although "the surf is vigorous and swimming is not recommended." In-room pet-and-owner massages are available as well and include over 140 different treatments. For instance, neck rubs help combat pet jet lag.

Room service "is delivered via a specially outfitted three-wheeled cycle," she goes on. "Sparky and Iggy could not believe their good fortune!" Along with menu items such as Ranch Dog Fantasy (cubed chicken and gravy) and The Rin Tin Tin (shredded braised beef and rice) served in metallic bowls with faux gem stones on bone-shaped place mats, the chef will prepare made-to-order meals. "The only repercussion...was that the boys thought every room service delivery thereafter was expressly for them." Oh, well.

Along with the usual shopping and dining—including the resort's two restaurants and tequila bar—human diversions include golfing, horseback riding, water sports, and boating. Pet sitting is available.

"Ruffing" It:
Backpacking, Hiking, and Camping

Planning an active or camping vacation requires additional legwork. Not only will you need to make sure Rover is permitted at parks, campgrounds, trails, and other nature areas, but you must carefully follow each facility's rules. For instance, only service dogs are allowed in many public buildings. Also, make sure "your dog is a model canine," states Cheryl S. Smith, author of *On the Trail With Your Canine Companion.* "Maybe you can convince a park manager to accept dogs that have a CGC (Canine Good Citizen®) certificate or an obedience title."

In an interview on the about.com Web site, she suggests including dogs in as many activities as possible. "[They] are a natural for the outdoors. They can be great entertainment," chasing moths around the campfire, using their attuned senses of sight and smell to notice deer, elk, moose, and other animals you might otherwise would have missed. "Contrary to the opinion of some land managers, the presence of a dog does not send wildlife heading for the far hills."

Ground Rules for a Safe and Hassle-Free Experience

❖ Call before making any plans. Requirements change constantly.

❖ Always let someone know where you're going and when you'll return, whether it's a ten-day camping trip or a short hike. Inform friends at home, park rangers, and other travelers who will be on the alert should you not come back on time. Cell phones are a good backup, but technology and coverage can be spotty in remote areas.

Planning a camping or hiking vacation with your dog requires prior research. Not only will you need to make sure pets are permitted at the parks, campgrounds, and other nature areas you'll visit, but you must carefully follow each facility's rules. Photo courtesy of DogGone Newsletter.

❖ Even if you're outside, always clean up after you dog. You never know where other hikers/campers will step!

❖ Most campgrounds and parks expect pets to be leashed at all times. Otherwise, animals should be crated or kept in a tent.

❖ Never leave your pet unattended, even when on a leash. Small dogs might be an attractive snack for wild things and even bigger pooches can't always defend themselves. Rover might also be stolen and/or harmed by two-legged critters.

❖ Learn about the poisonous flora and fauna in the area. This would include oleander, stinging nettle, cactus, poison ivy, and more. Have antidotes on hand in case Rover gets into it anyway.

❖ Should you be out and about in the wintertime, watch for puddles of antifreeze in parking lots. Even drinking a little can prove deadly.

❖ Regularly check your dogs for ticks, dehydration, and foot injuries. Paw pads can be particularly vulnerable to abrasions and soreness, particularly if you've done a lot of walking. Dog boots might be a good investment if you plan to hike extensively.

❖ Drink water from your personal stash and not a source found in the wilderness.

❖ After returning home, have your dog looked over by your veterinarian to make sure he's as healthy as when you left.

In the event of confrontations with wild and/or domestic aggressive animals, you can take several courses of action. Banging a large empty plastic soda bottle against your hand or other surface will make lots of noise and usually scares them away. A can of mild pepper spray is another legal and safe deterrent. "Bear bells" also serve as an advance warning system and can prevent those potentially lethal creatures from crossing your path. Should you run across a grizzly, there are several ways to circumvent an attack, the most prudent of which is to maintain a safe distance and nonthreatening manner. Others include standing your ground and avoiding eye contact, allowing the bear to "mock charge" and run past you, and playing dead. Make sure your dog is quiet and contained, even if you have to physically restrain him. (*Never* run or climb a tree because bears can do both much faster than humans and other animals.) Also bring odor remover in case your dog has a close encounter of the skunk kind. Otherwise, no one will want him around, including his owner!

Locating Parks, Camps, and Outdoor Areas

Many Web sites have state-by-state breakdowns of recreational areas. However, the following sites provide information on park and camping opportunities for you and your four-legged friend:

❖ *National Parks:* www.nps.gov; www.recreation.gov. National forests are more amenable to canines.

❖ *State Parks:* http://members.home.com/state-parks-online/

❖ *Directory of RV Parks/Campgrounds:* www.gocampingamerica.com

Backpacking and Hiking

Dogs have traditionally been beasts of burden, so why not let Rover range with his very own backpack? Of course, you wouldn't expect him to automatically go an entire day with a full load; start with a small towel, so your healthy, fully mature pooch can get accustomed to wearing something on his rear. (Putting loads on puppies under one year can result in damaging developing bones.) Begin with lightweight items and short walks and make it a fun experience, rewarding and praising your dog as he keeps the pack on for longer periods and discouraging him if he starts chewing on it. Your pooch should be in good physical shape, so lengthening "conditioning" outings before the trip helps build up endurance.

Along with loading the pack with things that can be easily replaced (water bottles, doggie toys, his and your snacks, and food), make sure the heft of the pack is evenly distributed, fits properly, and is no more than one-third of the dog's total body weight. Factors such as strength, size, and general physical condition should also be considered. Some "working" dogs can carry up to 50 percent of their weight, but only if they are in peak condition. And putting a backpack on a toy breed and expecting the dog to walk for hours is unrealistic, unless you plan on carrying him a good part of the time. It also might be wise to have the dog x-rayed for hip dysplasia, particularly if it's inherent in the breed.

Most campgrounds and parks expect pets to be leashed at all times. Otherwise, animals should be crated or kept in a tent.

Periodically check your pooch for signs of abrasion from the pack. If sores do occur, pad the area with soft fabric. Also remember that dogs like to romp in foul-smelling things and often go for a spontaneous swim in streams, so all items in the pack should be placed inside two heavy-weight plastics bags for protection.

Tenting/Camping

The good news about camping is that, unlike hiking, Rover can be more of a couch pooch-tato, so this is a fun option for older and less fit dogs. You can also take more supplies with you because you don't have to schlep them wherever you go. However, the only way to make it a happy camping experience is to abide by the rules of the site: along with basic doggie etiquette, this means no barking, leaving "deposits," or disturbing the other guests and their pets.

Along with a tent and the usual four-legged camping supplies, Rover will need something to sleep on (best bet: a doggie

Trail Safety and Etiquette

- ❖ *Always* keep Rover on a leash and under your total control at all times. Keep him quiet, contained, and calm when others are passing.
- ❖ The biggest animal always has the right-of-way. Step aside for livestock and horses so they won't get spooked. The pecking order on most trails is: everyone yields to large animals, bicyclists yield to joggers and hikers, and joggers yield to hikers. Some individuals are afraid of dogs, so let them pass as well.
- ❖ Watch for and avoid wild animals, as well as other dogs and small children.
- ❖ Keep to the right, the left is for passing. Downhill traffic yields to uphill hikers.
- ❖ Pay attention to the terrain and various descriptive signs; some have steep grades and limited visibility. Know the distance of the hike so you can pace yourself and your friend.
- ❖ Take frequent bottled water and rest breaks, being aware of your dog's body language. To do otherwise might result in heatstroke and injury. At best, you may have to carry your pooch for the duration of the trek.
- ❖ Stay on the trail and away from shortcuts, which can harm the land.
- ❖ Avoid swampy and muddy areas, slippery slopes and, in winter, deep snowdrifts and cross-country ski areas.

bed from home if it's portable enough); protection from the cold in the form of a blanket or a dog coat and booties; snake bite ointment, antibiotic, and other medical supplies, particularly if you're going far into the wilderness away from medical care; and a muzzle if he tends to be aggressive.

Cleanliness can be lifesaving at a campground, particularly if bears are around. No longer shy about raiding a seemingly unattended camp when they smell food, every year grizzlies maul and murder visitors in national parks and elsewhere. Therefore, burn all trash, remove leftover edibles from the site, and hang any items that have an odor, such as soap, garbage, and toothpaste, from a high tree away from the sleeping area. Dogs can be a good deterrent because they can make a lot of noise, keeping bears away from the vicinity.

Camp Pooch

Multiplying like the rabbits that Rover loves to chase, dog camps are among the trendiest and most convenient vacation options. Not only do they require a minimum of planning on your part, but there are many different kinds, with activities ranging from tail-wagging and kissing contests and dog-hair weaving classes to serious training in obedience and competition. Be aware, however, that some kennels and doggie day care facilities may refer to themselves as "camps," but actually aren't. A true dog camp offers a unique learning and relaxation experience for both of you and is more than a place to leave your pooch when you're out of town or at work.

Although each camp has its own "personality," they have some commonalities. Most are in bucolic settings—on beaches and lakes, near forests and park lands—far from the bustle of

When camping, check your dog regularly for ticks, foot injuries, and dehydration. Also, be sure your pet only drinks water from your personal stash and not a source found in the wilderness.

cities, with plenty of walking and hiking and small-town pleasantries. Although human meals and lodging are often included and are home-style and simple, you're generally expected to bring Rover's food, toys, and bedding (and possibly even the latter for yourself). Be prepared to share rustic (no private telephones, TVs, AC, or heat) quarters and bathrooms with your fellow campers; few places offer the amenities of a hotel or even a nice RV. As with hotels, camp-grounds, and other public areas, dogs must usually be crated when you're not with them and on a leash most other times. Owners are generally required to participate.

Barking Hills Country Club, Milford, NJ, 908/996-9911, www.barkinghills.com. Okay, so they don't have a golf pro or require dress whites for tennis, but they do offer a complete canine sports package. Agility, flyball, lure coursing, and carting are emphasized, along with obedience classes and pet therapy programs that prepare dogs and handlers to visit hospitals, nursing homes, and the like. Set on seven acres, of which four are surrounded by a six-foot, double-gated fence, you and your pet can stay at nearby dog-friendly hotels. However, classes are on a week-by-week basis, rather than being concentrated in a few days like most camps. So it's more practical for people who live nearby and can commute.

Camp Dances With Dogs, Lebanon, NJ, 800/735-9364, www.flyingdogpress.com. Activities ranging from psychodrama to hypnosis to agility help you get in touch with your inner canine. Although additional offerings include veterinary chiropractic, communication, tracking, behavior, and holistic care, "this is not a camp for folks who want rigid schedules or non-stop activities," states organizer Suzanne Clothier on the web site. "It's for folks who are willing to go beyond conventional thinking to explore what is possible between a human and a dog." Lest you think it hippy-dippy or New Age: "We emphasize depth of knowledge as the basis for humane training. There is plenty of laughter, but also tears as people work through some serious issues about relationships, themselves, and their animals." Clothier screens her applicants carefully: Your deposit (refundable only if you're turned away) must be accompanied by a detailed questionnaire.

Camp Gone to the Dogs, Putney, VT, 802/387-5673, www.campgonetothedogs.com. This perennial favorite is perhaps the most well-known of canine camps; Honey Loring, the director, has been in business since 1990. The 50-some activities per day, "big" (as in 210 people and their dogs) summer camp runs the full gamut: training, sports, grooming, massage, coping with behavior problems, and lectures on nutrition and health. And then there's "just plain fun"—a doggie costume party, hot dog retrieve where Rover's supposed to return the wiener uneaten (ha!), and arts and crafts. "Do it all, or just sit around, kiss your dog, and eat bon bons," states Loring. There's also a more laid-back mid-summer "mini" camp and a fall foliage camp. Summer camp starts in early June; mini-camp, late July/early August; fall foliage, early October.

Camp Winnaribbun, Lake Tahoe, NV, 775/348-8412, www.campw.com. You and your favorite companion can "bone up" on obedience and competing, as well as doggie sports like flyball, agility, tracking, and even swimming for water-averse pooches. There's also a field trip (so to speak) at a

Dog camps are among the trendiest and most convenient vacation options for you and your canine friend. They require minimum planning and provide activities ranging from tail wagging contests to serious training in obedience and competition.

nearby ranch to try your hand at sheep herding. Nature walks, homeopathy and healing techniques, and focusing on positive mental attitudes help round out events. Bonus: While Rover is asleep from exhaustion, you can do some gambling at nearby casinos along with other two-legged activities of golf, fishing, and parasailing. Held for one week, in early September.

Competitive Edge Sports Camp, Cornwall-on-the-Hudson, NY, 508/529-3568, http://members.aol.-com/CESCampfordogs. This experience focuses on serious "canine athletes and their people interested in agility, obedience, or canine disc," states the web site. It's limited to 170 dogs—no more than two per person—and 84 owners. You are asked to select a "major" for the week, and then grouped based on your pet's proficiency, with a 1:7 instructor-to-student ratio. Elective workshops include such subjects as impulse control (the dog's), versatility (the trainer's), and sports psychology, as well as private coaching, trials, and games. The nearby Black Rock Forest has plenty of walking trails, although there's no extra credit if your pooch catches a squirrel. The five-day, six-night program is scheduled for July.

Dog Days of Wisconsin, Waukesha, WI, 800/226-7436, www.dogcamp.com. This laid-back affair (hence the name) is open to all breeds and mixes, from puppies to octogenarians and beyond (in doggie years, of course). You can fill up your days with seminars on training, sledding, grooming, cooking, first aid, dental hygiene, arson investigation, or simply swim, do arts and crafts, or wander among the pines and play ball with your pooch. There's even a costume and pet trick contest (no David Letterman, though), and dog-and-owner partial and full-body massages. Camps run for two four-day sessions in August.

Dog Scout Camp, St. Helen, MI, 517/389-2000, www.dogscouts.com. "Be prepared" to have fun while learning lots of unique stuff. Activities include "naked" dog obedience without the use of a collar or leash; backpacking/hiking; the art of shaping, where you actually "teach" your dog to paint (let's see Letterman's pets try that one); and obstacle course training, including agility and flyball, in addition to water safety, search and rescue, wolf behavior, and bite prevention. You can also learn to make dog

Some summer camp programs offer a full range of long-term classes for those who can invest in a lengthier stay, including advanced training, sports, grooming, massage, coping with behavior problems, and lectures on health and nutrition.

cookies (for, not from, Rover), as well as try your hand at telepathic communication and massage. Merit badges and titles for achievement, skill-building games, contests, scavenger hunts, and crafts provide lots for Rover to chew on. Should he meet all the requirements, he might even become a Dog Scout with his very own picture ID and DSA added after his name. Two six-day, five-night camps are held each year in July in Michigan and one in August on the West Coast.

K9 Sports Camp, Northridge, CA, 310/838-7195, www.K9Sports.com. This condensed, activity-intensive happening concentrates on agility, flyball, disc, herding, musical freestyle, schutzhund, and more. There's also lots of fun stuff—musical mats and "Simon says" games, a campfire gathering—and a vendor showcase for the latest in accessories and duds. The three-day weekend winds up

A true dog camp offers a unique learning and relaxing experience for both you and your dog. This canine camper participates in a kissing contest with his owner. Photo courtesy of Camp Gone to the Dogs.

with competition and prizes and is generally held in mid-September.

Splash Camp, Monroe, CT, 203/372-0747, www.flyingdogpress.com. Founded by veteran police officer, animal photographer, and water dog champion trainer, Deborah Lee, this unique camp focuses on "the holistic approach to training a water service and companion dog," she states. Emphasis is on teamwork between "guardians" (her term) and their dogs, and "is based on understanding the whole dog—mind, body, soul, and individual needs." Specific areas of concentration include retrieving, towing, delivering, companion swimming, jumping and diving, as well as targeting people, places, and/or boats and directional control (i.e., come, go out, sit, etc.). Dogs must be in good physical and mental shape to participate. Beginners can get their paws wet at a pre-camp, which is held the Friday and Saturday before the regular program and emphasizes the basics.

More Camps

In the US:

- ❖ *The Dog's Camp, 7 Greenleaf Rd., Fletcher, NC, 828/684-4814.* Contact Catherine Mills, SkyeBCs@mindspring.com.
- ❖ *Legacy Behavioral Camps, Seminars, and Workshops, P.O. Box 3909, Sequim, WA 98382, 360/683-1522.* Contact Bill Ryan, blryan@olypen.com or Terry Ryan, teryan@olypen.com.

In Canada:

- ❖ *Camp Ruffin' It, Vancouver, BC, 604/439-8450.*
- ❖ *D.O.G. (Durham Obedience Group) Camp, Ashburn, Ontario, 905/434-6465 or 905/655-4314,* hkadish@sypatico.ca.

Alternative Transportation
and Non–US Destinations

Taking Rover with you off the beaten path, be it by air, rail, or sea, can be a real challenge and in some cases, a near impossibility. Amtrak, Greyhound, and other interstate bus lines prohibit pets, although some local rail and bus carriers make exceptions. (Perhaps Greyhound should change its name to "No Hound?") Should you try to sneak him in where he's not allowed, however, be prepared to spend some time in a big cage yourself—a.k.a. jail. At the very least, you will be fined and your pet may be confiscated.

Pets are similarly forbidden on cruise ships, except for the *Queen Elizabeth 2*, where they're restricted to the cargo hold, a bummer for your dog, making it a "guilt" trip for you. Nevertheless, canines may be permitted on smaller or private boat or on transatlantic "tramp ships," freight or merchant vessels that pick up cargo wherever they roam. Routes include the US, Canada, Europe, Egypt, and the Mediterranean. Running only during the warm months, these voyages often take 15-30 days or even more, depending upon the stops and port delays, so you'll need to be flexible about travel times. Some allow large dogs in the cabin and it can be a bargain, unless, of course, you get stuck somewhere. It's no luxury trip; the fee includes one sit-down meal a day with the captain and crew; the rest of the time you fend for yourself in the galley. Forget about aerobics, midnight buffets, passenger talent contests, and on-board massages and facials. For more information, contact the *Cruise People Ltd., 800/268-6523, http://members.aol.com/CruiseAZ/home.htm.*

Should you decide to sail with Rover, take certain precautions, such as making sure he's tethered to the deck and outfitted with a canine life vest with glow-in-the-dark sticks. Also, make provisions as to waste disposal if it's going to be more than a few hours.

An Excursion on the Magic Bus

Every rule has an exception, and this one's found on the Green Tortoise Bus Line, a throwback to the hippie-run companies of the 1970s. Dogs and owners are generally allowed on the West Coast Alternative Run, round trip from Los Angeles to Seattle.

Rather than the usual rows of torn, gum-infested seats, the big green buses boast comfortable booths and couches, converting to a big bunkhouse at night, with a few sort of "private" sleepers. Since most customers are laid back and many have dogs, your pooch can usually snuggle with you. Breakfasts are home-cooked, but you and your pet had better make a pit stop before getting back on, because the bus lacks a bathroom. Not to worry, it stops every two hours and the driver will pull over if the situation gets desperate.

Dogs are on standby until the driver makes sure that your pet is clean and people-friendly and that the other passengers are cool with having a canine on board. Many bring dogs themselves, but some folks do have allergies and phobias. Most of the time, it's not a problem.

Taking your dog with you off the beaten path—whether by air, rail, or sea—can be a challenge, and in some cases a near impossibility. For problem-free travel, be sure to research the regulations before transporting your pet across state or international borders.

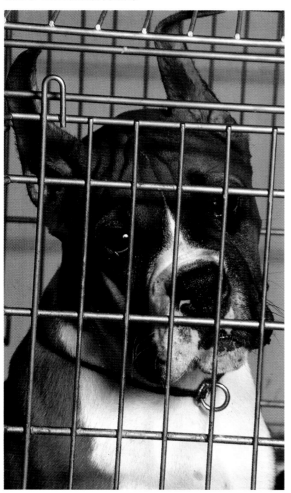

Although itty-bitty pooches are half fare, most dogs must pay the full price. *Green Tortoise Bus Line, 494 Broadway, San Francisco, 800/867-8647, www.greentortoise.com.*

Those wanting to avoid the hassle of planning their own trip might do well to hook up with *Rovin' with Rover, 888/757-4584, www.rovinwithrover.com.* Proprietor Janice Wenig leaves the driving and other details to her enterprise, which organizes one-day tours and hikes throughout various places in Ohio, including Hocking Hills, Amish country, and Marietta; the Chautauqua region in New York; the Allegheny area and Cornfield Maze in Pennsylvania; and Niagara Falls, Canada, among others. She's also willing to take groups of 20 or more on longer legs to dog-friendly destinations like Dollywood, Williamsburg, Greenfield Village, Quebec, Toronto, and more. Each pooch gets his own seat next to his master in a plush tour bus. Meals generally consist of a box lunch or outdoor seating in a restaurant. "I foresee more pet travel companies popping up," she says on her Web site. "Perhaps there will eventually be hotels that only accept people with dogs!"

Air Travel

The viability and safety of dogs flying is a source of dispute. Some folks find it potentially deadly, particularly if the pet travels in the baggage or cargo hold, while others regard it as less dangerous than driving. The truth lies somewhere in between: As long as you follow certain rules, the chances of Rover arriving in the same condition as his owner are 99 percent, according to the Air Transport Association of America (ATA), which estimates that half a million pets fly a year.

Often, booking your dog's ticket can be more complicated than yours and generally involves a moderate to expensive fee for larger canines, sans frequent flier miles, of course. If

Dogs must be at least eight weeks of age before they are permitted to fly.

you're going overseas, it will obviously be more costly. Shop around: Sometimes even different personnel at the same airline will provide varying prices and policy. So make sure you get the name of the individual whom you've talked with, as well as documenting the information.

This is where a travel agent comes in handy. Also, for a fee, shipping services provide coordination for the transport of pets, including health certificates, import permits, special licenses, and customs clearance. Mostly utilized for relocation, they might be particularly helpful if you're traveling separately from Rover or are going overseas. (*O 'Brien Animal Transportation & Services [OATS], 650/348-0547, www.animaltransportation.com; Jet Pets, 800/738-8901.*)

Additionally, each airline has particular specifications for crates and kennels. But before making that first reservation, consider the following questions.

❖ *Is my pet fit to fly?* According the Animal Welfare Act (AWA) administered by the United States Department of Agriculture-Animal Plant Health Inspection Service (USDA-APHIS), dogs and cats must be at least eight weeks of age and weaned for five days before liftoff. Tiny puppies, dogs that are very old, pregnant, in heat, or sick should not fly. Felines, snub-nosed breeds (Pugs, Boxers, so on), and dogs with long snouts like Collies and Shelties may have respiratory difficulties in the cargo hold and should travel in the cabin with their owners.

You might also want to consider an alternative form of transportation if you need to tranquilize your pooch. Groups such as the American Animal Hospital Association (AAHA) and other pet and air transportation organizations recommend against it. Along with possible breathing and heart problems in both cabin and cargo from increased altitude pressure, sedated animals may be unable to brace themselves when carriers are moved, resulting in injury. Those with short, wide heads are particularly vulnerable to disorientation. "Airline officials believe that when deaths occur they often result from the use of sedation," states Dr. Patricia Olson, DVM on the AAHA web site. And although some studies state that only one percent of animals in cargo are harmed or killed, that's still some 5,000 pets, according to animal rights groups.

However, Congress recently passed a law that now requires airlines to make monthly reports on passenger pets that are lost, injured, or die. Training must also be improved in handling animals as well. The maximum allowed reimbursement covered by airlines' luggage loss/damage policy has

Each airline has different policies regarding pets traveling in crates and kennels. For example, aside from proper documentation, some require that your dog be fed and watered four hours prior to departure.

also been doubled If misplacement, injury, or death does occur, register complaints with *USDA-APHIS, 4700 River Rd., Unit 84, Riverdale, MD 20737-1234, 301/734-4981, www.aphis.-usda.gov.*

❖ *How will my pet fly?* There are three options: as a carry-on in the cabin (your canine should be no more than 11-16 pounds, although some airlines allow up to 18 pounds), in

Airline Contacts

Air Canada, 800/776-3000, aircanada.ca
Alaska Airlines, 800/426-0333, alaska-air.com
America West, 800/235-9292, americawest.com
American Airlines, 800/433-7300, americanair.com
Canadian Airlines, 800/426-7000
Comair, 800/354-9822, fly-comair.com
Continental, 800/525-0280, flycontinental.com
Delta, 800/221-1212, delta.com
Northwest, 800/225-2525, nwa.com
Southwest, 800/495-9792, iflyswa.com
TWA, 800/221-2000, twa.com
United, 800/ 241-6552, ual.com
USAirways, 800/428-4322, usair.com
(All Web sites prefaced with "http://www" unless otherwise noted.)

the climate-controlled baggage hold, or as cargo. The first two generally occur if you're traveling with your pet, and the last if the animal flies alone and usually requires arrangements through the cargo department of each airline. The latter should also be avoided, because without overseeing the situation directly yourself, snafus are more likely to occur at either departure or destination. Dogs and kennels weighing more than 100 pounds might even have to travel on a separate plane as air freight, so check this out with the ticketing or travel agent before purchasing the fare.

Unless pets are carry-on, animals are classified as luggage and as such may be loaded on the plane via conveyer belt. Should the carrier fall off the belt, your pet could be injured or released. So ask if Rover can be hand-carried on and off the plane and if you can watch both activities (before deplaning, remind the flight attendant to notify the baggage handlers that you're on the way to observe your dog being unloaded). Another alternative is "counter-to-counter" shipping, when the pet is placed on the plane immediately before departure and unloaded right after arrival. This may cost a bit extra, but it's worth it.

Although carry-on pets are not covered, the AWA does enforce the humane and safe treatment of animals elsewhere on the plane. For example, dangerous goods like chemicals are supposed to be in a different part of the hold than live animals. Some airlines are less stringent about this, so call beforehand to discern exactly where your dog will be placed. If you carry your dog on the plane, make sure his container fits underneath the seat in front of you, that it's comfy and roomy, and that he remains well-behaved and quiet. Inform your seatmate(s) that you have a pet, so they or you can switch if need be.

❖ *What are the regulations?* Each airline has specific policies, although all are subject to the AWA. Most only allow two to seven pets per flight, so you'll need to book early. And although it's hard to control the type of aircraft you'll be flying on—this can also change shortly before departure—try to stay away from DC-10s and narrower jets like Boeing 727s and 737s, which have limited air circulation. Wide-bodied aircraft such as Boeing 747s and the French-built Airbuses do provide heated/air-conditioned cargo holds. All are pressurized, of course, but those without forced air can heat

When traveling, it's a good idea to carry a clear recent photo of your dog to distribute in case he becomes lost.

up more quickly than the cabin if flights are delayed.

Different airlines have various standards of care, so it's important to do your homework and thoroughly investigate each one. In general, the more information they provide, the better your pet will be treated. Ask if the workers have been instructed or at least accustomed to dealing with animals—this is now a legal requirement. Talk to other dog owners who've flown with their pets and get their feedback as well.

Rules for small or commuter flights may differ so make sure you know with whom and what kind of plane you'll be flying in. And sometimes it's good news: For instance, Nantucket Air, Cape Air, along with Air France's Concorde allow large dogs in the cabin, with certain stipulations. However, airlines also change their guidelines frequently, so check with them 24-48 hours before you leave. Should your canine be traveling in the hold, inform the gate agent so he/she can ensure that Rover is indeed on board.

❖ *What will the flying conditions be like?* The airline reserves the right to refuse to transport your animal for any reason, be it health, climate, or simply because the dog seems agitated. The AWA prohibits animals in the uncooled/heated hold if the ground temperature is less than 45 degrees or above 85 degrees; some airlines even impose tighter restrictions, forbidding pets to fly to cities where the temperature might exceed these limits. So, in summer, fly in the early morning or late evening when it's cooler and in winter, during the warmer middle of the day. Also, try to fly "off peak" (i.e., not on holidays or weekends) when crowds are smaller and delays less probable.

Let the pilot and flight attendants know that you have a dog on board the plane (showing a picture of Rover generally melts even the hearts of the petless.) Should you be stuck on the tarmac for more than 30 minutes, the danger for heatstroke or hypothermia increases. Ask flight personnel if they can activate heating/cooling in the hold, if necessary and available. You should be allowed to check on your canine should this situation arise.

Also, reserve a nonstop flight or, at the very least, stay on the same plane, particularly if your dog is placed in cargo. Not only does this reduce the chance of potential delays, but it eliminates the possibility that Rover might be accidentally rerouted to Poughkeepsie instead of Puerto Vallarta. If there's no other alternative, find out where to go to retrieve and re-board him during the aircraft change.

An exception would be a flight more than nine hours. Then you might want to schedule it in two segments, with a layover midway. You can "fetch" Rover, feed him, and take him for a walk. However, travel-acclimated dogs do fine on longer international flights of ten hours or so.

❖ *Are you prepared?* Before flying, make sure you've done the following:

Get a certificate of health from your vet no more than ten days before departure. Like your driver's license, you'll need to show it at the ticket counter.

Clip Rover's nails so they won't get hooked on any part of the carrier.

Feed and water your canine before departure. Each airline has a different policy as to when this should occur, although with food, it's generally four hours before and with water, it can be any time. You'll also need to sign documentation as to when you last fed him. Regulations vary as to whether or not food and water are permitted in the kennel, but, if allowed, use dry food and freeze water so it can melt by the time the flight is underway.

Along with a sign saying "Live Animals," clearly and boldly label the carrier with your name, address, phone number (home and where you'll be staying), and the dog's name. Directional arrows need to indicate proper positioning of the kennel. Your canine should also have an identifying collar. Attach additional food and a leash to the outside of the kennel in the unlikely event that your dog gets misrouted.

Your dog's "passport" for international travel will include a certificate from your vet testifying to his good health completed no more than ten days before departure, along with necessary medical documentation for shots and other treatments.

Line the bottom of the kennel with some type of bedding to absorb accidents. Soft paper towels are good. You also might want to include something familiar so Rover can have a reminder of home while in the air. Don't be surprised if there's a "present" waiting for you at your destination, so bring supplies to clean it up.

Unless you're traveling with hamsters—the USDA allows 50 per crate, although there may be more by the end of the trip—it's best to have one dog per kennel, unless the animals are extremely small or are compatible (i.e., live together or are littermates).

Arrive at least one but not more than four hours before departure. If Rover is traveling as carry-on, check-in is at the passenger terminal; but if traveling as cargo, you'll need to go to the cargo terminal, usually in a different part of the airport. Regulations vary from airline to airline if your dog is going as checked baggage. Check with the airline as to where you'll need to drop him off, as well as the acceptance cutoff time for your flight. Then give yourself a few minutes extra.

Exercise your dog outside the terminal just before the flight. Make sure he "does his business" in a place away from human and other traffic.

Keep your canine in his carrier at all times, unless requested otherwise by airline personnel. If you must remove him, for example, when passing through security on your way to the gate, make sure he's firmly leashed. Bring along a muzzle just in case your pooch freaks out.

International Travel

Canada

Traveling with your pet back and forth across the border should be hassle-free, although you will need a certificate from your vet testifying as to Rover's good health, as well as written proof of rabies shots within the past 36 months (collar tags are considered insufficient). Make sure the vaccination doesn't expire while you're on vacation, because the same documentation will be needed to get back into the US. If you're entering from a country other than the US, be prepared to pay a fee at the border for veterinary inspection.

There are a couple of exceptions. Puppies under three months that are too young to vaccinate can get a certificate from the vet stating this, and dogs entering through Newfoundland require a certificate and entry permit, to be obtained in advance. For more information, contact the *Canadian Food Inspection Agency (CFIA), in eastern Canada, 905/612-6282; in western Canada 604/541-3370.*

Everywhere Else

Those planning to travel abroad need to prepare for a lengthy flight and, at best, a short quarantine period. Even Hawaii has 30- and 120-day quarantines, and it's in the United States! The longest quarantine, six months, is still required by the United Kingdom, but this can be circumvented thanks to recent changes in certain criteria. Unfortunately, dogs coming from the US and Canada still do not qualify. And New Zealand requires mandatory microchip implanting with a minimal scan fee at its borders. Having the correct currency on-hand will also prevent your pet from being confiscated.

Your canine's "passport" will be a certificate for International Movement of Small Animals from your vet, to be completed no more than 10 days before departure, along with the necessary medical documentation for shots and other treatments, if necessary. If you plan to keep Rover out of the country for more than 30 days, check with the airline/destination to see if you'll require additional certification while abroad.

Although France has no quarantine, other European countries and Australia aren't as pet-friendly. Most isolation periods range from 1-6 months; book accommodations in advance with the country's officially run or approved kennel. Contact the embassy or consulate of the place you'll be visiting (most are based in Washington, DC) and get their requirements for documentation and quarantine. That should minimize unpleasant surprises—such as having your pet taken away from you, put in "solitary confinement," or in extreme cases, destroyed—and you and Rover can enjoy your exotic experience together.

Pet-Friendly (and Not So) International Destinations

The following countries welcome dogs (no quarantine, but require papers/vaccinations):*

Caribbean:
Aruba
Bonaire
Caicos Islands
Guadalupe
Punta Cana
St. Barts
St. Marrten/St. Martin

Europe:
France
Italy
Switzerland

United States territories:
Puerto Rico
US Virgin Island (includes St. Croix, St. John, St. Thomas)

Long quarantines, lengthy application process, tough restrictions:

Caribbean:
Anguilla
Antigua
Bahamas
Barbados
Jamaica
St. Kitts/Nevis
St. Lucia
St. Vincent

Europe:
Ireland
United Kingdom

United States:
Hawaii

* Some are subject to change and final verification

Sitter or Stayover?

Sometimes there's no other choice: You must leave Rover behind. And this can be a good thing, especially if you select the right kind of care. What may work for a quiet dog that is accustomed to being on his own may be a disaster for a friendly Fido that prefers nonstop stimulation. So it's up to you, the owner, to figure out what's best for your pet(s).

Kennel or Sitter?

If you are going on a trip and must leave your dog at home, there are two options: a kennel or a pet sitter. In recent years, kennels have enjoyed a renaissance. The 1977 establishment of the American Boarding Kennels Association (AKBA) resulted in the development of a set of standards, a code of ethics, and a certification track and now boasts 1600 operator members throughout the US and Canada. Also, with an estimated 9,000 kennels servicing over 30 million pet owners annually, doggie boarding accommodations come in almost as many gradations as human hotels, from bare-bones runs 'n cages to all-the-trimmings private suites, complete with TV, VCR, and Web-based software so concerned owners can log on and see Rover at play.

In general, the kennel is a better selection for "animals that need medical supervision...that become bored or stressed when left alone...(leading to destroying the house, barking, etc.)," writes Janet Tobiassen Crosby, DVM on the about.com Web site. "The kennel is also more 'social' so for pets that enjoy the company of others, this is a nice option to keep them busy."

Another advantage: Boarding facilities are designed to prevent your pooch from going AWOL. At home, he might escape from a friend or inexperienced sitter who is watching him to try to "find" you. At a kennel, he has no other choice but to stay put.

However, thanks to such groups as the National Association of Professional Pet Sitters (NAPPS), Pet Sitters International, and resources like the Pet Sitters Yellow Pages, you can be assured of getting quality in-home care just about anywhere in the US. Some sitters may even take dogs into their domiciles; but for purposes of this discussion, they should be considered the same as a kennel.

Photo courtesy of The Kennel Club.

If you are traveling and must leave your dog behind, there are two options for care: a kennel or a qualified pet sitter.

With a sitter, your canine remains in his own environment and remains free of exposure to diseases or potentially unfriendly animals, alleviating that nagging sense of "What's he doing now? Is he okay?" Along with giving him fresh food, water, walks, and affection, the sitter will watch the house, take in the mail, and turn lights off and on to deter burglars. But things can and do go wrong—the animal may become sick or something might happen to the residence, such as a flood or fire, when the sitter's not around. Rover can also get into unsupervised mischief. The ideal sitter would be there around the clock, but these are rare and very costly. Most sitters visit for about an hour at least twice daily. This is an ideal solution for the multi- or mixed-pet household, where animals can entertain each other and saves on boarding costs.

What you *never* want to do is leave your dog "home alone"—even if it's only for a couple of days. That's an invitation to trouble. Not only is he likely to destroy things out of anger, boredom, and frustration, but you'll be punishing him in the worst way possible. Even the most laid-back canine depends upon his two-legged companions for social and physical needs.

Choosing a Kennel

There are several ways to locate a kennel, but the best resources include recommendations through a trusted vet or dog-owning friends who've left their pet at the facility themselves. Some clinics allow boarding in addition to providing medical services. But evaluate these as you would a kennel, because you never know what goes on while the cat (or in this case, the owner) is away. Kennels can also be found via the ABKA, your local Better Business Bureau, and as a last resort, the Yellow Pages. With the latter, "the size of the ad is no indication of the facility's quality," cautions the ABKA Web site.

First, call the kennel and see if they can accommodate your dog. This should be done several weeks or more in advance, because kennels book up quickly during Christmas, summer, and other holidays; even weekends can be tough. You might want to make reservations at several places so you have a "spot" for Spot. And should you decide against a particular facility, don't forget to cancel your booking as soon as you make your choice.

Next, case the joint. Ask to see the areas where the animals will be exercising and staying, although you may not be allowed total access due to precautions against contagious diseases and upsetting the boarders. You can come back at a time when the section is not being used; some kennels provide a viewing window so you can see where your pet will be staying. An unscheduled stop at another time during hours of operation will offer additional insight as to how things really run. Other considerations include the following:

❖ *Appearance/Sanitation.* Is the kennel clean? A well-maintained building can be older and still neat and in good repair. Are the woodwork and linoleum well-scrubbed or is there dirt caked on and debris lying about? Does each new tenant's space get cleaned and sterilized? Is there freshly washed bedding? Ask about a schedule of disinfecting, which can prevent diseases such as parvovirus.

Overall, what is the smell? Remember, with pets around 24/7, expect some accidents and an unpleasant whiff or two. But if it's one of stale urine or old feces, or wafts into the manager's office while you're talking, cross the kennel off your list.

And what about the kitchen? Are the dishes washed and provisions stored properly? Is the dogs' food and water fresh, rather than stale-looking and scummy?

❖ *Amenities.* Are the assigned quarters large enough to comfortably accommodate your pet? Are they well-ventilated to minimize the spread of bacteria and diseases? What kind of bed will your dog sleep in? Will the temperature be within Rover's comfort zone? If he's older or has particular needs regarding cooling/warmth, see if special arrangements can be made.

Can dogs "socialize" with each other during playtime? Dogs and cats should be kept separately to help eliminate aggressive behavior and excessive vocalizing. Do exercise areas provide shelter from wind, rain, snow, and direct sunlight?

Can Rover get that special attention he needs, even if it's a daily brushing or personalized walk? That will give him something to look forward to.

❖ *Security/Safety.* Fencing, gates, and run dividers should be sturdy and well-maintained. Exercise areas that include high barriers between

There are several ways to locate a kennel, but the best resources include recommendations from your vet or other pet owners who have boarded their animals.

runs prevent male dogs from urinating into adjacent runs. Do inside runs have latches that lock? Do outside runs have enclosures that prevent homesick pets from jumping over the wall? If your dog is a climber, digger, or other type of "escape artist," tell the kennel operator so additional precautions can be taken. Surfaces also need good traction even when wet.

Kennels areas should be free of sharp objects, harmful chemicals, and objects that might be swallowed. Sleeping quarters should provide solid dividers between your pet and the other boarders, both for reasons of safety and so Rover can relax without feeling challenged or distracted by neighbors. Fire-fighting equipment should also be available.

❖ *Supervision/Activities.* Find out about feeding schedules and activities. How often and where are the dogs walked? How is the kennel laid out in terms of runs and exercise facilities? Designs range from indoor/outdoor runs, totally enclosed quarters, and inside housing and outside exercise areas. Ask the operator to explain the uses and benefits of each so you can make the most informed decision concerning your pet.

❖ *Healthcare/Personnel.* What kind of treatment will Rover receive if he gets ill? Will the kennel be able to get him to a veterinarian, preferably yours? If it's affiliated with a veterinary hospital, are the sick animals kept away from the healthy ones? If you're not asked to provide up-to-date medical records, then take your dog elsewhere, because there's a risk of contagious diseases.

Have the staff taken any professional medical care courses? Are they trained to recognize signs of illness such as loss of appetite, sneezing, lethargy, and bloody stools? Are they pet owners themselves? Is there a veterinarian on 24-hour call? Many kennels will turn down animals requiring potentially dangerous procedures like diabetes shots or excessive medication that needs to be given more than three times per day or throughout the night.

❖ *Business Practices.* Are the days and hours of business clearly posted? Many kennels are closed on weekends or holidays, so plan arrivals and departures around that.

Rates should be available in the office. Be sure that you understand the method of calculating boarding charges. Some have a checkout time, after which you must pay a full day, while others charge by the hour or blocks of time. Get information about extra costs like heartworm pills and flea baths so there won't be any "surprises" when you are presented with your bill. Expect to pay more if any additional medical/veterinary treatment is needed.

The kennel should have a boarding agreement, which clearly states your rights and the kennel's responsibilities. This protects everyone involved from misunderstandings. Is the facility a Certified Kennel Operator (CKO) and/or accredited with the ABKA? This guarantees a designated standard of training, ethical treatment, and service.

For more information, contact *The American Boarding Kennel Association (ABKA), 4575 Galley Rd., Suite 400A, Colorado Springs, CO 80915, 719/591-1113, www.abka.com.*

Preparing for a Kennel Stayover

❖ Drop off and pick up your dog at the prearranged times during business hours. Make sure he's been walked to avoid accidents during the tumult of leaving him.

- Bring a towel and plenty of his toys to remind Rover of home. Spend time with him before taking him to the kennel, so he doesn't feel neglected.

- If the kennel doesn't use Rover's food, give them enough to last the stay. Also provide a leash, even if he's usually walked without one.

- Supply kennel personnel with a list of phone numbers where you can be reached at all times, including the number of his veterinarian.

- Be up front and honest about Rover's character traits: for example, if he's a biter or aggressive, or vomits frequently. Otherwise, you'll get phone calls and complaints, and he may not be allowed back. Most kennels are understanding and will make accommodations, as long as they know what to expect.

- Make sure your dog is up to date on his meds, including vaccinations (bordatella, coronavirus, par-

Along with a well-trained and kind staff, a good kennel should provide individual cages, indoor/outdoor runs, meals on your own dog's schedule and with his diet, clean bedding, and medical care if necessary.

vovirus, and so on) and heartworm. If needed, your pooch should also have plenty of special medication on hand, as well as instructions as to dosage and information on situations or food that might upset his system.

- Your dog must be recently bathed and flea-free.

- If he is not already, make sure your pet is accustomed to being handled and walked by strangers, as well as being crate trained. If the dog is young or has never been boarded before, ask if you could leave him for a "test run" night or weekend to see how he'll adjust.

- Never act upset when you walk away from Rover. Hugs and tears will only stress him out and make adjustment more difficult. The kennel operator may ask you to leave him in the office rather than having you place him in the run. That way, he'll realize that you've entrusted him to the kennel's care. Hold your emotions until you get back to the car.

When you return:

- Ask about Rover's stay. How did he adapt? Did he display any unusual behavior or require special handling? This information will not only be entered into the facility's records for future use, but can be helpful should you board your dog at another kennel.

❖ Try to wait four hours before feeding and watering. Your canine needs to be completely calm; otherwise he may "wolf" (woof?) down his food, which may trigger vomiting or diarrhea. At best, offer a few ice cubes when you first get home.

❖ Expect Rover to be "pooped." After the initial excitement of returning home, many dogs sleep almost continuously for a day or two. However, if you observe anything out of the ordinary, immediately contact the kennel operator.

Simple vs. Deluxe Doggie Digs

A "no frills" kennel is the most affordable, depending upon the size of the dog. With a kind, well-trained, and knowledgeable staff, Rover can do quite well with regular food and exercise and a watchful eye for illness. These kennels include individual cages, indoor-outdoor runs, meals on your dog's own schedule with his own diet, clean bedding, medical care if necessary, and several daily inspections to make sure he and the other tenants are thriving. They may also charge a bit extra for giving daily medication or providing a bath and/or flea dip.

But if you want to treat Rover like a king, a "doggy resort" might be just the ticket. This option can be quite pricey. Services can consist of pick-up and delivery service; intake examinations; pre-check-out grooming and washing; personalized walks; special housing, particularly if the dog is sick or elderly; plush accommodations, including bedding and toys; a lounge and exercise area that allows them to roam free in a contained space; and "classes," such as obedience training. Some add-ons and amenities may alleviate the owner's guilt rather than enhancing the dog's experience or sensibilities. For example, your pooch won't likely be as impressed with a TV in his room since he's color-blind anyway and only has a limited command of English.

Doggie boarding accommodations come in almost as many gradations as human hotels, from bare-bones runs and cages to all-the-trimmings private suites. Photo courtesy of The Kennel Club.

The following are a few facilities that stand out in the pack.

Almost Home Kennels, Putnam Valley, NY, 914/528-3000, www.almosthomekennels.com. Located on 24 wooded, double-fenced acres—the better to be contained in—accommodations are completely air-conditioned in the summer and have radiant heat in the winter. Private indoor/outdoor chambers boast off-the-floor sleeping platforms. The 24-hour-a-day piped in music and security system directly connected to local police and fire departments make this an ideal retreat for the discriminating dog that wants to get away from it all.

The Kennel Club/LAX, Los Angeles, CA, 310/338-9166. With on-site gourmet picnics in the park, theme cottages well-stocked with doggie videos, story time, de-stressing massages, and even a class in weight reduction, this is Rodeo Drive, Rover-style. For a few dollars more, your pupness can stay in the VIP suite in the night attendant's apartment, bed privileges included. There's also 24-hour drop-off and pick-up so you don't have to worry if your plane's late.

Kennelwood Village, St. Louis, MO, 314/429-2100, www.kennelwood.com. Six-by-nine foot luxury suites are individually decorated and have picture windows that allow spacious views of the grounds. There's a play school for walks, fetch, and tetherball, as well as all the brushing, petting, and attention that owner's can afford. Things wind down with daily "Yappy Hour" and dog-friendly cookies and ice cream.

PETsHOTEL PLUS, Tuscon, AZ, 520/323-2275, www.petshotel-plus.com. This all-indoor "inn" with an atrium and gourmet meals can be a real holiday. With kids' beds, ceiling fans, cable TV(!), and private phones that allow Rover to hear his mistress's voice whenever she calls, the suites really put on the dog. The rest of the population stays in private rooms—if you have multiple canines, they can share—and are reached out and touched by owners who call via a public booth in the atrium. Other goodies: "Yappy Hour" with a non-lactose frozen Dogarita and biscuits, and treat-filled Bizzy Bones that may cause your dog to "hound" you to pick one up in the retail area.

Triple Crown Dog Academy, Hutto, TX (near Austin), 512/759-2275, www.triplecrowndogs.com. This 350-acre former ranch is for real he- (and she-) dogs. Indoor/outdoor runs, rubber floors that are easy on paws, three-sided paneled accommodations, all may bring out the wolf in even the most refined Miniature Poodle. However, touches like piped-in music, custom meals with doggie ice cream, and a whirlpool-like bath offer indulgent touches after a tough day of working with a professional trainer, romping the grounds, and swimming lessons. Even older pets may learn a few new tricks while you're away.

Two Dogs and a Goat, New York, NY, 212/631-1157. Park Avenue pooches—or those who can afford it—can bypass the entire bourgeois kennel concept and stay in staff members' homes. They're cooked for, walked, and escorted to their regular assignations by pet-care providers who intimately know every animal-friendly store, tree, fire hydrant, and park in the neighborhood. Other services include obedience training and caring for young, elderly, and sick animals.

Other innovative canine lodgings abound. Although overnight guests sleep at a nearby veterinary clinic, *The Big Backyard, Denver, CO (303/757-7905, http://www.the-big-backyard.com)* has 7500 square feet with three indoor playrooms, two fenced yards, and a doggie lounge. *Bed & Biscuit (212/475-6064, www.bedandbiscuit.com)* in New York City is an actual B&B limited to a handful of pups and offers weekend trips to wooded "Woofstock Acres." Located on in an old farmhouse, the folks at *Fly N Hy Kennels* (651/455-0364, *www.fly-n-hy.com*) in Inver Grove Heights, MN, recommend not bathing Rover so he can get down and dirty in the pasture and play area and he still sleeps inside the home. The appropriately titled *Dog-Ma Daycare* (203/543-7805, *www.dog-ma.com*) has the only cageless overnight digs on Capitol Hill in Washington, DC (not available to legislators in the "doghouse," however). *Central Bark, Los Angeles, CA* (310/285-0070, *www.lacentralbark.com*) provides web cams and high-speed DSL lines so owners can view their canines in "real time" on the Internet. Owned by Bart "Dog Boy" Emken, *DogBoy's Positive Power Kennels* (877/467-6837, *http://www.dogboys.com*) in Pflugerville, TX, offers a football-sized fenced-in area for all-day play for compatible dogs, a "swimming hole" (actually a large tank), and distracting music during those Texas-sized thunderstorms.

Choosing a Pet Sitter

Despite the ever-evolving array of kennels, pet-sitting is still a viable option, particularly if you're from a city or upscale suburban area. The key here is finding the right sitter, both for you and your canine. What works for one person may not for another—for example, a quiet, grandmotherly, stay-at-home type may have a difficult time with your gregarious 65-pound German Shepherd that loves to romp and roll.

Although family, friends, coworkers, and even veterinarians can provide resources, you might also want to research members of various professional pet-sitting organizations and listings in your area. This can be done either by telephone, e-mail, or the Web. Many affiliates are experienced, trained, and do this for a living.

As with a kennel, you'll need to call well in advance, particularly if you're traveling on a holiday, school vacation time, or over a long weekend. You might need to interview several sitters before you and your buddy latch onto the right one. When meeting the sitter for the first time, ask the following:

With a reliable pet sitter, your canine remains in his own comfortable home environment and receives individualized care and affection.

❖ What is included in the fee?

❖ Are you insured for commercial liability and bonded? Ask for proof.

❖ Can you provide three references? You, as an owner, must check them out.

❖ What kind of transportation do you have? Can you take Rover in the car, if need be?

❖ How long have you been doing this? What kind of animals do you typically care for?

❖ Do you know how to handle a medical, weather, or home emergency?

❖ Can you take care of special needs regarding medicine or food? Can you, for example, "pill" a dog?

❖ How much time a day will you spend with Rover? When and how often will you visit?

❖ What are your contingency plans if you happen to fall ill? Do you have a substitute or backup?

The pet sitter should have:

- ❖ A standard contract outlining terms of service.
- ❖ References.
- ❖ Questions regarding your dog's medical history and recent vaccinations. He should insist that all shots be current.
- ❖ A sincere interest in Rover's temperament, health, schedule, and needs. Pay close attention to how he interacts with your dog. Does he seem to genuinely love animals? How do they get along?
- ❖ A professional, confident, and competent attitude and demeanor.
- ❖ An affiliation with, or at the very least familiarity with, pet-sitting associations and organizations.

Locating a Pet Sitter

Check with these resources for a list of pet sitters in your area:

National Association of Professional Pet Sitters (NAPPS)
1200 G St. NW, Suite 760
Washington, DC 200005-4797
800/296-7387
www.petsitters.org

Pet Sitters International
c/o Patti Moran
418 E. King St.
King, NC 27071
336/983-922
www.petsit.com

Pet Sitters Yellow Pages (online only)
www.petsitters.com

Follow your own and your animal's instincts. If Rover doesn't like the sitter at the first meeting, go on to the next name on the list, no matter how highly he's been recommended. A couple of additional visits so your dog can get used to the sitter as well as familiarizing him with the house and its idiosyncrasies (for example, where's the mop in case of an accident?) are well worth the additional effort and expense.

Be forthcoming about your dog's good and bad habits, favorite hiding places and escape tricks, and health issues. Along with a signed release allowing him or her the power to approve emergency medical care, you'll also need to provide a list of phone numbers: where you'll be staying, the vet, neighbors in case the sitter needs to contact them, and service people like the electrician, plumber, and house cleaner. Keys and written-out instructions should be in his or her hand before you leave, along with a readily available supply of your pooch's food and water, dishes for same, leashes, and favorite toys and treats. Before you go, make sure Rover's where he's supposed to be and remind the sitter that his collar and tags need to remain on him at all times.

You should never leave your dog home alone for an extended period. Even the most laid-back canine depends on his two-legged companions for his social and physical needs.

Essentials for the Pampered Traveler

The Internet, catalogues, and retail stores offer an almost dizzying cornucopia for the cosseted canine. These can range from flavored tennis balls, doggie breath freshener, and oat straw pet soap from *Two Girls and a Dog (404/373-7898, www.2girlsandadog.com)* to gift baskets stuffed with toys, waste disposal bags, ear cleaners, and more commemorating the major fire hydrants in Rover's life *(The Dog Basket, 630/679-0630, www.thedogbasket.com).* You can chart out the "dogography" for your and your pet's itinerary at *Map Adventures (802/ 253-7489, www.mapadventures.com)* or record Rover's movements (well, not *every* one) in a pet diary and photo album *(Four Paws Publishing Group, 604/803-8490, www.fourpawspublishing.com* and *Dog's House Gift Catalogue, 800/851-6899, www.dogs-house.com).* "Pet passports," which contain pictures and health, identification, and travel records, are even available *(Snyder Smart Systems, 619/442-2650, www.pet-passport.net).*

Your pooch can obtain personalized scarves, fleece throws, and towels from *K9Design (800/684-7181, www.k9design.com);* that doesn't even include the dozens of accessories and crafts sold to owners. And those who want details on decorating a doggie domicile might do well to purchase Fred Albert's *Barkitecture*, a book that showcases 50 unique animal abodes throughout the US.

Most cities and tourist areas have at least one specialty store that's "gone to the dogs" with pet supplies, treats, and wearable art. A nearby PetsMart or PETCO offers discounts and often welcomes Rover inside.

Crates and Carriers

Certain items are basic for travel with your dog. One of the most important is a proper crate and carrier. It serves your pet equally well both on the road and in the air and is a sort of "home away from home" in providing a sense of comfort and familiarity. Dozens of types and styles abound.

For hotel and other travel needs, standard plastic or metal carriers usually perform the trick. They can be found at just about any pet store. Most consist of a top and bottom plus a gate, all of which can be quickly and easily assembled or taken apart. Also look for the following, which are required by most airlines:

- ❖ The crate must be enclosed, but with ventilation in a minimum of 14 percent of the wall space. The top half should be at least one-third open-air. It needs an outer "lip" or rim of 3/4" surrounding the exterior to prevent blockage of circulation.
- ❖ The crate must open easily, but must be sufficiently strong to hold up during cargo loading and unloading.
- ❖ The floor needs to be solid and leakproof and covered with an absorbent lining or material (such as a towel).
- ❖ The carrier should be large enough for Rover to turn around and have full range of motion. Remove all objects that might cause harm during movement (such as loose dishes or hard toys).
- ❖ Exterior grips are necessary so handlers don't have to put their fingers inside and risk getting nipped at.
- ❖ Wheels must be removable or at least immobilized prior to loading and when the dog is alone in the room.

Road Trip Accessories

One major automobile company, Saab, has recognized the necessity of the safety of pet travel. In conjunction with the Humane Society of the United States (HSUS), they've developed a line of vehicle accessories for their station wagon, including a seat belt, a specially designed restraint system for the cargo area, as well as a cargo guard and space divider for same. A pet harness also fits around the dog's neck or torso for safe retention and doubles as a leash for walking outside the auto. (For more information on these and other offerings contact your local dealership or the Saab Web site, *wwww.saabnet.com.*)

For the Grr-eat Outdoors

Comfort and fit are vital in purchasing canine back and side packs, which have enjoyed increasing popularity. Not only do they need to be large enough to carry the proper load, but they should allow plenty of ground clearance and enable Rover to lie down, even when the pack is full. Straps should be wide and soft, with one going under the dog's torso and the other in front of his chest. You might need a spare to put around the haunches or below the tail when hiking on rugged terrain or steep descents. Straps should be secure, but loose enough to insert your finger beneath them. At first, inspect them often to make sure they remain consistently in place. Once your pet gets used to the pack and it's properly adjusted you won't need to check as often. For older and less mobile doggies and pups up to 18 pounds, you can purchase a front-mounted, infant-style carrier, which is easy on your back.

Certain items are basic for travel with your dog. One of the most important is a proper crate or carrier, which protects your pet both on the road and in the air and serves as a home away from home providing comfort and familiarity.

Life jackets provide a welcome margin of safety when taking Rover sailing, white water rafting, or swimming. Some combine buoyancy with a secure and natural fit, along with a grab handle, and reflective trim for maximum. Other designs comes in fluorescent colors and have a strap for pulling Rover out of the water, making this useful for boating and other situations where he might get caught in the undertow.

Back on land, you might want to protect your pooch's delicate paw pads with booties, particularly when doing lots of hiking. However, they should be used judiciously: over rocky or abrasive terrain, to cover an injured paw, or when traveling over snow. They can also be worn inside the tent to prevent the dog's claws from tearing the interior. However, it is recommended that you toughen the dog's paws naturally and frequently check the booties for signs of wear and tear.

Dog-Friendly Treats

All that exercise can make a pooch hungry. Available from many catalogues and pet stores as well as directly via phone order and online, dog-friendly treats can be given before, during, and after a workout or hike. A balance of natural sugars, simple and complex carbohydrates and premium oils, they come in beef, chicken, and peanut butter flavors.

Happy trails!

Index

Photo Credits

Alexis Hotel, 25

Wendy Ballard, 27, 28, 32

Camp Gone to the Dogs, 39

The Chesterfield Hotel, 7

The Kennel Club, 50, 56

Honey Loring, 39

Janice Wenig, 8

All other photographs by Isabelle Francais